LEADERSHIP &
ORGANIZATIONAL
CULTURE

LEADERSHIP & ORGANIZATIONAL CULTURE

A Multi-Step Program for Success

DR. DENNIS R. CLODI

WITH

DR. RICHARD SCHUTTLER

authorHOUSE®

AuthorHouse™
1663 Liberty Drive
Bloomington, IN 47403
www.authorhouse.com
Phone: 1-800-839-8640

Published by AuthorHouse   05/23/2013

ISBN: 978-1-4817-5441-5 (sc)
ISBN: 978-1-4817-5440-8 (hc)
ISBN: 978-1-4817-5439-2 (e)

Library of Congress Control Number: 2013909331

Any people depicted in stock imagery provided by Thinkstock are models, and such images are being used for illustrative purposes only.
Certain stock imagery © Thinkstock.

This book is printed on acid-free paper.

CONTENTS

ACKNOWLEDGEMENTS

I want to acknowledge my close professional colleagues/friends who have always counseled and encouraged me to do more writing. I don't need to list your names—you know who you are.

There are some very special people I want to acknowledge. I want to acknowledge Dr. Rich Schuttler, for encouraging me to take my work as an organizational consultant and share my work with the world. I want to acknowledge Dr. Ruby Rouse for editing this book for us. Dr. Ruby is a sincere, caring person who has been an inspiration to me since I have gotten to know her through our work at the university where we both teach. Thank you so much Dr. Ruby for being there for me.

One very special professor I had during my doctoral program needs to be acknowledged for the great influence he had on my life during and after my degree program. Dr. Paul Baker, a retired Illinois State University professor, challenged my thinking and writing every day. He not only taught me content, but taught me both the practical and theoretical side of what to do with that content. I will be forever grateful to Dr. Baker.

Lastly, I want to acknowledge Connie, my wife of 49 years, for allowing me take time away from being with her while I wrote this book. I want to thank her for passing up many personal and professional opportunities so I could pursue mine. My two children, Jeff and Michelle have always been beside me, encouraging me to continue my work, and writing. Without the support of these three people, I probably would have not accomplished most of what I have done in during my life. Without their love and support, I would never have completed my doctorate much less writing projects like this one. I love and thank the three of you very much for all your help, belief in me, and your constant support.

This Book

Is

Dedicated with all my Love to

my 9 year old granddaughter Faith

Without Faith's constant smile, positive attitude, and reminders to Grandpa not to let the stressors of the world get him down, this book would not have been possible.

✓ As a former senior Air Force officer leading many large organizations and now a business executive in corporate America, I have seen first hand the effect an engaged leader has on implementing necessary changes. Doctors Clodi and Schuttler have developed a roadmap that does not detail "what to think", but, rather, outlines "how to think." For any leader to embark on organizational change, he/she would be well served by following the guidance herein . . . . you'll be glad you did!

Greg Power, Major General, United States Air Force (retired)

✓ To succeed in a competitive marketplace, organizations must be capable of fluid, dynamic, and effective change. Clodi and Schuttler's *Leadership & Organizational Culture: A Multi-Step Program for Success* empowers you with an intuitive process to prepare, implement, and follow up on change initiatives. Using a blend of case studies and self-reflective exercises, you'll learn about leadership, vision/mission statements, communication, conflict, and change implementation.

Before you can change your organization, you must change yourself! Embrace the lessons in *Leadership & Organizational Culture* to accelerate your success!

Ruby A. Rouse, Ph.D.

✓ This book is a great guide for leaders to follow when managing change. Many leaders tend to think change is an event that just happens. Managing change in an organization is a process that takes time, planning, buy-in from stakeholders, and follow-through. Explaining the two types of changes in an organization, cultural or structural, Clodi and Schuittler have created a clearly written and easily understood product. All organizational leaders should invest in this book and use it as a source to manage change.

Dr. Ron Heuss, retired public school administrator and county official.

✓ Drs. Clodi and Schuttler have worked with me on a variety of organizational problems. I know from experience their approach to making cultural changes in organizations works. If your organization is looking to change the culture successfully, following the steps they have included in this book is a must read.

Dr. Genova Singleton, Singleton and Associates, LLC.

✓ As a consultant, educator and executive, I have seen far too many change efforts begun as a reaction instead of a carefully considered process. Clodi and Schuttler have created an integrated framework of questions, examples and strategies that support successful change by considering all facets of organizational and leadership requirements. Avoid the "ready, fire, aim" phenomenon; invest in this experience-based approach!

April Flanagan, CEO, April Flanagan & Associates, Inc.

INTRODUCTION

———

Leaders or Boards of Directors often believe the culture of their organization is in need of change. Sometimes the organizational culture is in need of change; other times it is not. In today's global marketplace, it is important for leadership to make the right decision.

There are proven success steps leaders need to follow to bring about cultural changes in their organizations. This book provides the steps and questions for leaders to address relative to whether their organizations are in need of a change. It asks leaders to consider their leadership style, to look at what other organizations have done, to set goals and timeframes, the organization's vision and mission statements—all before making a final decision about whether there is a need for changing the culture.

The importance of effective communications can make the difference in whether an organization succeeds in changing. Too often leaders believe providing information about how an organization is changing is the same as communicating how and why an organization is changing. Nothing is further from reality. Followers need to understand how organizational changes will affect them personally.

Because many followers are not comfortable with change, conflicts often arise. This book discusses how organizational leaders can foresee and prevent some conflicts from happening and how to deal with the conflicts that do arise.

Lastly, the book outlines the steps leaders need to follow to ensure a successful change in their organizations. Too often leaders do not outline a plan of action the leads to a successful change. Without a plan of action, leaders often don't stay the course, ensuring failure of the organization.

The authors hope leaders will find this book a useful guide as they work through the process of deciding whether change is needed and how to implement the change once that decision is made.

Thank you for purchasing this book.

Dr. Dennis R. Clodi
Dr. Rich Schuttler

LEADERSHIP

Part 1 in a Series of 5

There are proven success steps leaders follow to bring about cultural changes in their organizations. This book offers ways to facilitate successful organizational change. Questions are also provided to help ensure positive outcomes where measured goals and objectives are created and then tracked to completion.

As a leader, it is important for you to understand that the speed of organizational change is directly related to the size of an organization. **CHANGE TAKES TIME.** Planned change, with proper implementing and tracking strategies, allows goals to be realized. To make informed decisions about the need for a cultural shift, you must first look at what currently exists inside and outside of your organization. Then you should include other stakeholders to develop a sound and systematic approach.

PLANNING A CHANGE EFFORT

There are 3 major steps to consider:

- ➢ Preparing for Change
- ➢ Implementing Change
- ➢ Following-up on Change

Each step in the change process requires careful and detailed planning. If any step is done incorrectly, organizational resources may be lost, time wasted, and morale affected.

There are several questions that must be addressed before you begin:

- ➢ Do I have a compelling reason to justify the change?
- ➢ Have I identified the key stakeholders to discuss the possible change?
- ➢ Am I prepared to make a strong personal commitment to the change?
- ➢ Am I ready to handle change-related disruptions that may occur in my organization?
- ➢ Do I have a timeline prepared for making the changes?
- ➢ What will my organization's new vision/mission statement be after the change?
- ➢ Do I have the resources needed to implement the change?
- ➢ Have I prioritized the steps needed to successfully implement the change?
- ➢ Am I prepared for potential casualties that may occur during/after the change?
- ➢ How am I going to communicate the planned changes to everyone involved?
- ➢ What communication channels are available for my team members to use?

DOES MY LEADERSHIP STYLE MAKE A DIFFERENCE?

Leaders must take an honest look at how they manage their followers and stakeholders. The more *autocratic* a leader has been in the past, the more difficult it will be for followers to trust the changes he or she wants to implement. Those leaders who have led with a *transformational* leadership style will often find it easier and faster to garner support from the followers during a shift in the culture of their organization. Transformational leadership is finding ways to help followers perform beyond expectations their superiors and their own personal goals. Transformational leaders are concerned with all aspects of their followers' personal and professional lives.

Based on your current knowledge, what is my current leadership style (transformational, transactional, charismatic, authoritarian, servant, situational, other)?

_____

_____

_____

_____

If I decide to make a cultural change in my organization, will I need to modify my current leadership style? If so, how? If not, why not?

_____

_____

_____

_____

What tools and resources are available to me and my leadership team members to analyze our current leadership styles?

Do I have these tools or resources available internally? Yes   No

If NOT, do I have the financial resources to find outside help? Yes   No

THE INSIDE LOOK

In today's rapidly changing business environment, there are products and services that were not available a few short years ago. If a leader would like to expand a product/service line to retain the organization's competitive advantage, he or she may need to make changes within the organization. Leaders, along with their teams, will need to evaluate the results they hope to see, examine the current culture and procedures of their organization, and determine if their current strategy still makes sense. More importantly, a leader must realize the status quo may no longer be working. Leaders must be willing to abandon processes that do not yield results and search out other opportunities that will prove successful.

As you contemplate whether or not a change is needed, don't accept the idea that your organization has gone as far as it can. Doing so creates an immediate barrier to greater success. Effective leaders are visionaries who regularly consider how they can improve their organizations—increasing revenue, decreasing expenses as well as gaining greater efficiency and effectiveness.

A holistic plan to deal with significant change in personnel, vision, mission, and values must be put in

Leaders must be willing to abandon processes that do not yield results and search out other opportunities that will prove successful.

place. If current stakeholders are expected to change, they must understand the new paradigms—and they must be given a reason to believe the new paradigms will work.

Those who choose to come onboard must be assured that they are making the right decision. Many may hear negative feedback from others who are resisting the changes. Such individuals need reassurance about their job security. It is important for the organization to provide a safe environment for workers to express questions and concerns.

Leaders need to make a strong personal commitment to follow through once the change process has started. They must understand that most followers dislike and resist change. If they waiver in their resolve to change, leaders often lose credibility, trust, and possibly their jobs. Leaders should only begin a major change if they are committed to it and can endure negative feedback that might arise.

Leaders must determine whether outside human resources will be needed to make the changes envisioned and if the organization has the financial ability to hire outside consultants. These issues need to be addressed prior to any changes being implemented. A monitoring system also needs to be in place to determine where the organization is with regard to the planned changes.

There are two kinds of changes organizations can make—structural and cultural. Structural changes can be simple or difficult, depending on the size of the organization and/or the level of change being considered. Structural changes can be as easy as moving people into new or different positions—or they can be difficult if people or positions are being eliminated. Both structural and cultural changes require followers to understand why the changes are being made and how the changes will affect them personally.

Change is personal and it affects everyone involved to some degree. Don't assume everyone in the organization is happy with changes even if the change seems to be logical and agreed to by all. Unhappy people have the potential to destroy morale or cause other problems that can hurt an organization. Most change plans fail when not planned adequately, and others fail because the change was implemented too quickly. Our experience shows when change is made, 30% of the followers accept it. Another 30% won't accept it and will either leave, attempt to undermine the change, or be terminated. The remaining 40% will watch from the sidelines until they decide whether they support the change and new vision.

If you believe your organization needs to change its culture or structure, vision, and/or mission statement, take time to think through the steps involved, and consider the issues that usually arise. Share your thoughts with your direct subordinates and other stakeholders to be sure you have the correct information that is guiding your understanding of the need for change.

What reasons have my leadership team and I identified that would motivate us to change the culture or structure of our organization?

_____

_____

_____

_____

What policies, practices, products, and/or services might we have to abandon if we change the culture in our organization?

THE OUTSIDE LOOK

Organizations are created to serve various stakeholders—customers, clients, patients, and/or students. Leaders need to identify how a cultural shift in their organization may affect those they serve. Is a change going to provide any value-added products? Have those being served asked for new products or services that can reinforce the need for a cultural shift? Does the organization have the resources to provide new products or services if a change is warranted? Looking at these outside considerations and answering these kinds of questions helps convince internal followers about the value of the proposed change.

What new products or services have our stakeholders requested?

_____

_____

_____

_____

_____

How (if at all) will the people we serve be affected by a change in the culture of our organization?

_____

_____

_____

_____

_____

What value-added products and/or services will we be able to provide our stakeholders if we decide to change the culture or structure of our organization?

_____

_____

_____

_____

_____

WHAT CAN LEADERS LEARN FROM WHAT OTHERS HAVE DONE?

For decades, experts have studied what leaders have done in successful organizations. Effective organizations have several things in common: they have few rules, the control is in the hands of the followers, and there are measureable standards. The followers trust the leaders. The followers are allowed to *own their own jobs*. The leaders in these kinds of organizations trust their people, empower them, and want to see them grow both professionally and personally.

CASE STUDY

In Bay City, Michigan, a 70-year-old General Motors (GM) parts production factory employed 4,000 people and was losing millions of dollars each year. Productivity was low, workers were demoralized, and they had no part in decision-making other than what their Union Local negotiated for them. Workers had to check in and out, not just at the beginning and end of a shift, but also to use the restroom and take required union-negotiated breaks. If an employee became sick during their shift, he or she was required to have a form signed by their immediate supervisor and the factory manager before being allowed to leave.

When asked about the factory's manager, the vast majority of workers said they had never met, nor even seen, the manager. Most didn't even know the manager's name. General Motors had plans to retool the factory, but the financial losses and low productivity made that plan impossible to implement. In 1986, 2,000 employees were terminated. With the loss of 50% their workforce, GM began to plan for a complete shutdown of the factory.

The GM leadership, hesitant to lose the factory, attempted to turn the losses and productivity around by hiring a new factory manager. In 1986, Pat Carrigan, a high school psychologist, was hired on as the new factory manager. Soon after Pat arrived, she walked the floor to introduce herself and shake hands with every employee. She told them she would welcome their ideas and comments and that they should feel free to seek her out at any time. Her immediate goal was to build mutual trust between herself, the employees, and the union.

While some plant managers viewed unions as an impediment to progress, Carrigan saw this as an opportunity to create a new partnership. The union chairman called Carrigan his partner. When someone complained about a decision Pat made, the chairman would tell them "it wasn't *her* decision, it was *their* decision and all decisions were made jointly by Pat and the union for the well-being of all employees."

Carrigan immediately involved the floor supervisors and union chairman in decisions regarding the employees, operating policies, negotiations with vendors, financial decisions for the plant, and working directly with customers. The employees quickly began to trust Carrigan because she was open with them. Soon employees were able to sign themselves in and out without permission. They set their own production benchmarks, kept their own records, and measured their own progress toward those benchmarks. One year later after these changes were implemented, a supervisor who had completed a computer report of his division's productivity progress proudly shared that, "*these were his records—he owned them.*"

Within two years, the plant was back on budget, productivity had skyrocketed, and the operations saved 13%—without a single employee laid off. Based on significant improvements, GM abandoned its plans to close the factory.

When Carrigan was asked what she knew about building auto parts, she replied she "didn't know anything about auto parts, but she knew her employees did and that was the only thing that mattered." When asked about her leadership style, she said, *"People are my thing!"*

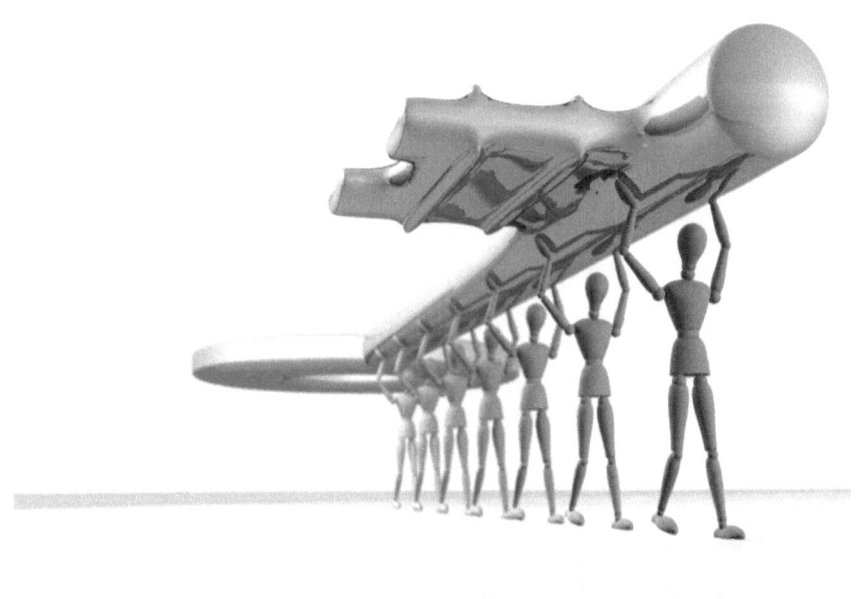

WHAT DOES PAT CARRIGAN'S LEADERSHIP STYLE MEAN TO ME?

Leaders contemplating a cultural or structural change in their organizations need to believe in their people (as Pat Carrigan did). Many leaders don't realize people are their greatest asset. Making crucial decisions without regard for employees, customers, patients, and other stakeholders is a strategy for failure. Finding those most trusted people in your organization and involving them in the change process is a strategy for success!

What can I learn from Pat Carrigan about changing the culture and structure of an organization?

_____

_____

_____

_____

_____

_____

_____

_____

_____

_____

_____

_____

_____

SETTING GOALS

WHAT IS MY LEADERSHIP TEAM TRYING TO ACCOMPLISH BY CHANGING THE CULTURE AND STRUCTURE OF OUR ORGANIZATION?

A goal should be measureable and realistic, yet not too easily accomplished. Goals may be long term and broken down to smaller, incremental steps. For example, quarterly goals contribute to a larger annual goal.

➢ **List measureable goals** you can track to monitor progress toward your objective. A measurable goal can determine if you are getting closer to your goal or further away from it.
➢ **Be specific!** Include a NUMBER that can be regularly measured to gauge your progress.

What specific, measureable goals can our leadership team use to assess progress toward our objectives? (Use additional paper if necessary.)

1. _____
2. _____
3. _____
4. _____
5. _____

Examples:

➢ Reduce injuries by 25%
➢ Improve customer satisfaction by 30%
➢ Obtain $50,000 line of credit

➢ Run a full marathon (26.2 miles)

ESTABLISHING TIMEFRAMES

Timeframes hold people accountable for achieving a measureable goal.

➢ **Select a realistic target date.** Do not procrastinate by setting a long window of time to accomplish your goal. But also do not expect miracles overnight!

➢ **Choose a specific date.** Organizations often have quarterly and annual dates for goals to be accomplished. For example, a deadline of December 31, 2013 could be established for a 12-month goal starting in January 2013.

By what date does my leadership team want to achieve our measureable goal?

Month, day, and year: _____

What is our rationale for selecting this particular date?

_____

_____

_____

_____

Examples:

➢ September 1, 2011-Beginning of the fiscal year
➢ April 7, 2012-Published deadline to submit proposal
➢ May 16, 2011-The date of a sporting event

➤ November 5, 2011-The date you desire to achieve a health or fitness goal

WHO IS RESPONSIBLE FOR ACHIEVING THE GOAL BY THE DEADLINE?

It is important to designate one key member of the leadership team who is accountable for making sure each measurable goal is accomplished. This person may personally oversee the accomplishment of the initiative and/or function as a team leader for the organization.

Goals are rarely achieved by one person alone. More frequently, the assistance and participation of others at work or home (maybe both) are required.

Whose help does our leadership team need to accomplish our goals?
1. _____
2. _____
3. _____
4. _____
5. _____

Examples:
➤ Sales employees
➤ Business consultants
➤ Managers

Who are the most trusted members of our leadership team? List their names and current responsibilities.

1. _____
2. _____

3. _____

4. _____

5. _____

How will our leadership team monitor the progress of the new organizational change?

_____

_____

_____

_____

Who are other key stakeholders in my organization that need to be involved when implementing the change?

_____

_____

_____

_____

OTHER LEADERSHIP CONCERNS

Do I have the INTERNAL resources needed to successfully implement the change?

Yes   No

Will I need EXTERNAL resources in order to implement the change?

Yes   No

Do I have the FINANCIAL resources needed to make a change?

Yes   No

If our leadership team determines that a cultural change is necessary, what <u>internal</u> resources will we need?

_____

_____

_____

_____

If our leadership team determines that a cultural change is necessary, what <u>external</u> resources will we need?

_____

_____

_____

_____

If our leadership team decides to make a cultural change in our organization, what <u>financial concerns</u> do we need to consider?

_____

_____

_____

_____

NOTES

_____

_____

_____

_____

_____

_____

_____

_____

_____

_____

_____

_____

NEXT!

Vision & Mission Statements

VISION & MISSION STATEMENTS

Part 2 in a Series of 5

Most organizations have a vision statement—the dream or purpose of the organization. One reason followers may be reluctant to support a change is that the majority of them don't understand the organization's vision. They might not even know a vision exists. Despite the fact that they fail to communicate their organizational vision to their followers, many leaders expect followers to accomplish the organization's mission statement (the actual steps to make the vision come true). If followers are unaware of the organization's vision, it is no wonder employees struggle to achieve the mission statement.

ORGANIZATIONAL REALITY

One reason followers may not know their organization's vision might be that few vision statements make an impact. Another explanation might be that the vision doesn't align with what is actually taking place inside the organization. Leadership teams must be prepared to communicate a new vision and the accompanying mission statements differently than has been done in the past. For a cultural shift to be successful, followers must understand the vision or purpose of the organization and the mission statements that define how the vision of the organization will be accomplished.

If followers don't understand their role in an organization, any new changes are likely fail. Before change takes place, leaders need to inform followers of how their performance expectations will change. Followers will want to know if basic things like salary and benefits will be affected. It is the leadership team's responsibility to communicate this information.

What is the <u>current</u> vision of my organization?

_____

_____

_____

_____

_____

_____

_____

With the help of your trusted leadership team, draft a <u>new</u> vision statement for your organization.

_____

_____

_____

_____

_____

_____

_____

Based on the new vision statement, what changes need to be made to our mission statement?

1. _____
2. _____
3. _____
4. _____
5. _____
6. _____
7. _____
8. _____
9. _____
10. _____

How will our organization's new vision and mission statements need to be communicated to followers and other stakeholders?

_____

_____

_____

_____

_____

Who will be responsible for communicating the new vision and mission statement?

_____

_____

_____

_____

_____

What method of communication will those listed above be expected to use to ensure followers know and understand the new vision and mission statements?

_____

_____

_____

_____

_____

What timeframe will we use for communicating the new vision and mission statements?

_____
_____
_____
_____
_____

Who will be responsible for insuring the timelines are met?

_____
_____
_____
_____
_____

How will I adjust the timelines if initial benchmarks are not met?

_____
_____
_____
_____
_____

NOTES

_____

_____

_____

_____

_____

_____

_____

NEXT!
Communications

COMMUNICATIONS

Part 3 in a Series of 5

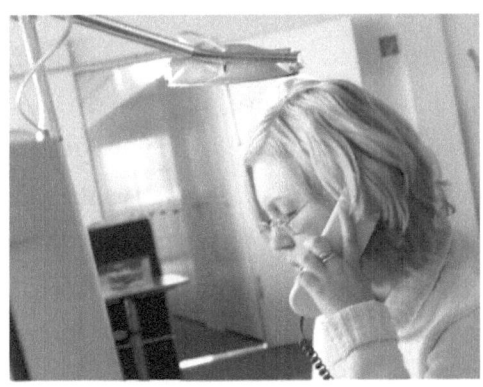

Despite all that has been published about effective communication, few leaders do it successfully. This often results in the 'blame game' being played. As organizational troubleshooters, we have found the number one reason employees quit their jobs is due to poor relationships with their supervisors (Schuttler, 2010).

It is often noted that technology has increased the ability to communicate. While it might be true that technology can provide an opportunity to increase an organization's ability to communicate, it rarely has. Rather, technology often provides new vehicles to abuse worker relationships and to send mixed messages.

"Communicate, communicate, communicate, and then communicate just a bit more!" This motto would appear to be simple, yet for most of us, it is difficult to do effectively on a consistent basis. Why don't we communicate effectively, especially when we've been communicating our entire life? Poor communication is an element common to organizations struggling to preserve a productive and effective workforce; the same poor communication is also found in many failing personal relationships.

> *"Communicating is far more complex than the simple sender-receiver model, as it involves real people with actual needs, wants, and differences."*
>
> —*Richard Schuttler*

The role of every leader in an organization is to effectively communicate vision, mission, intent, and philosophy. In an ideal workplace, communication is regular, clear, effective, and active, rather than missing or strained. Great communicators have common qualities that contribute to their strong leadership styles. Once these qualities are seen and realized, one can begin to incorporate them into their own skill set and leadership style. Good leaders provide a vision that is practical and achievable. A great communicator has the ability to create a shared vision that attracts others to their cause.

People often refer to U.S. President Ronald Reagan as "The Great Communicator." His communication style was effective, and he had the ability to persuade people to believe in his vision. He passionately described a better reality by simply suggesting, "The best is yet to come." Several eulogies at the former president's funeral mentioned his effective communication skills.

Table 1.1 contains statements made at President Reagan's funeral. While all these characteristics were credited to Reagan, they are shared by other historical leaders who created an atmosphere of trust—allowing people to work together for a common purpose.

Table 1. Communication Characteristics of President Ronald Reagan		
Made easy jokes with reassurances	Always maintained grace under pressure	Turned enemies into friends
Was candid, yet he often had tough words	Exhibited gentlemanly conduct	Gave a clear invitation to a new beginning
Put humility before honor	Held straightforward convictions	Avoided bigotry & prejudice
Was politely-stated	Loved a good story	Conveyed strength & gentleness
Possessed steadiness & calm	Maintained cheerful confidence	Exhibited elegance & ease
Demonstrated inspirational conduct	Offered humor & laughter	Acted on behalf of values & ideas

With practice, these characteristics can be learned and applied. Newly promoted supervisors, as well as seasoned organizational leaders, can learn to communicate more effectively as they gain confidence in their roles. As with any skill, practicing communication skills leads to greater levels of success and increased confidence. In turn, this confidence creates clarity of thought in both verbal and written dialogue, thereby reducing conflict.

> *"The problem with communication . . . is the illusion it has been accomplished."*
>
> *—George Bernard Shaw*

We have found that a significant relationship exists between how a supervisor communicates with an employee (one-to-one) and the worker's resulting performance. We also believe there is a relationship between how an organization communicates with all its employees (the organization-to-all-employees) and the organization's resulting performance.

When a leader tries to improve how an organization communicates, the *first* area to address is supervisors-subordinate communication. This is the first area to be addressed because it directly influences employee performance. The *second* approach focuses on how communication occurs collectively within an organization.

The inability of a supervisor to communicate effectively with one or more subordinates frequently results in confusion. The outcome can be a stressful work environment that negatively impacts productivity and employee retention. The resulting employee behavior often shows up as resistance to change and resentment toward organizational leaders. It is a supervisor's responsibility to communicate with each subordinate clearly and effectively.

- ➢ **We communicate our entire life!**
- ➢ **We admire great communicators:**
  - Parents
  - Grandparents
  - Teachers
  - Mentors/Coaches
  - Athletes
  - Leaders/Supervisors

Who are some people I believe are successful communicators?

_____

_____

_____

_____

_____

What are some of the characteristics that make them effective communicators?

_____

_____

_____

_____

_____

What characteristics do I possess that make me an effective communicator?

_____

_____

_____

_____

_____

What actions might I take to improve my communication effectiveness? (Examples: Self-awareness, observation of others, etc.)

What are barriers that may prevent me from being an effective communicator?

Survey results from the *2004 Economist Intelligence Unit* show that out of 276 senior executives in the United States and Canada, only 43% rated their companies as successful at carrying out strategic plans over a three-year period. The executives cited communication between senior management and front-line employees as the biggest challenge to ensuring effective communication. Interestingly, they also noted that this part of the business was "the most important to get right." In 2005, Kaplan and Norton noted that, on average, 95% of employees are unaware of, or do not understand, their organization's strategy. This statistic is alarming since it is the front-line workers who communicate directly to an organization's customers, stakeholders, or patients.

Chief executive officers (CEOs) agree that communication is an important management role that contributes to the success of their organizations (Moorcroft, 2003). Yet many organizational assessments suggest there is disconnect between how senior leaders, mid-level managers, and front-line workers assess communication.

Collectively, these statistics are consistent with the work we have done—work that details the symptoms of ineffective organizational communication. This is found throughout all industries and in all organizations—small, medium, and large. It is the role of an organization's leadership team to make sure effective communication is achieved and maintained. Organizational leaders have the responsibility of and are accountable for influencing employee performance.

Communication Tip: Practice Your Listening Skills

Do you often find your mind wandering when someone else is speaking? It happens to everyone now and then, but it's important that we all learn to really listen to other people.

Here are a few suggestions that will help you become an active listener:

- ➢ *Look at the speaker directly.*
- ➢ *Put aside distracting thoughts as soon as you become aware of them.*
- ➢ *Nod occasionally.*
- ➢ *Smile and use other facial expressions.*
- ➢ *Note your posture and make sure it is open and inviting.*
- ➢ *Encourage the speaker to continue with short verbal comments.*
- ➢ *Reflect what has been said by paraphrasing (e.g.," What I'm hearing is," and /or "Sounds like you are saying").*

➤ Ask questions to clarify certain points. *"What do you mean when you say . . ."* or *"Is this what you mean? . . ."*

➤ Summarize the speaker's comments periodically.

➤ Don't mentally prepare your response while the other person is speaking.

➤ Avoid being distracted by environmental factors, such as side conversations or people walking by.

What happens in organizations when the leadership team fails to maintain effective communication to mid-level and front-line employees?

_____

_____

_____

_____

_____

What steps might I take to improve communications between mid-level and front-line employees at my organization?

_____

_____

_____

_____

_____

_____

REACTIVE AND PROACTIVE COMMUNICATION

➤ **Reactive Communication**—Periodically responding to the lack of appropriate communication
➤ **Proactive Communication**—Regularly maintaining internal communication
  - Listening
  - Speaking
  - Asking questions
  - Sharing feedback
  - And more . . . !

REACTIVE AND PROACTIVE COMMUNICATION EXERCISES

What are examples of <u>reactive</u> communication in my organization?

_____

_____

_____

_____

_____

_____

What are examples of <u>proactive</u> communication in my organization?

_____

_____

_____

_____

_____

_____

Successful communication between employees results in increased satisfaction and higher morale. Best practices and organizational performance tracking reflect that, when organizational leaders manage and lead communications as a process, organizations experience decreased levels of anxiety and stress, along with rising productivity and job satisfaction. These same organizations report greater levels of employee commitment, declines in absenteeism, and decreased employee turnover.

Organizations often fail to carry out successful change for two reasons: lack of openness from leaders, and/or failure to engage employees when executing business strategies.

What other information should be communicated to all stakeholders?

_____

_____

_____

_____

_____

_____

Who will be responsible for communicating the information listed above? List each person and their individual responsibilities.

_____

_____

_____

_____

_____

_____

For each person you listed above, identify the timeline for accomplishing the communication to the stakeholders.

_____

_____

_____

_____

_____

_____

Who will be responsible for insuring that the timelines have been met?

_____

_____

_____

_____

_____

_____

How will I adjust the timelines if initial benchmarks are not met?

_____

_____

_____

_____

_____

_____

How will my leadership team communicate differently with employees once a cultural shift in the organization begins?

_____

_____

_____

_____

_____

_____

NOTES

_____

_____

_____

_____

_____

_____

NEXT!
Dealing with Conflict

DEALING WITH CONFLICT

Part 4 in a Series of 5

For many organizations the most difficult part of cultural shift is when people are asked to change, they often respond with comments like, "That's not the way we do things here," or "We've tried that before and it didn't work." They may resist the change in a variety of ways, including outright insubordination, undermining policies and directives, and simply refusing to do their jobs.

THE COST OF CONFLICT TO THE ORGANIZATION

Conflict in the workplace is not only stressful; it can hurt your bottom line. The cost of conflict to the organization is higher than you might imagine, and the trickle-down effect can damage your profits as well as the infrastructure of your business.

Let's take a look at how costly conflict can be, and the variety of ways it can manifest itself.

Lower Productivity Rates

When employees are faced with conflict in their daily jobs, they dread coming to work. This can translate into them taking more "mental health days." It can also mean employee performance rates suffer. Instead of concentrating on the task at hand, employees focus on the problems they are experiencing.

Each individual deals with conflict in his or her own way. Avoidance is, unfortunately, a popular technique that can result in higher absentee rates and inattentive or poor performance. Other employees may create disturbances, causing everyone else to feel awkward and stressed. When one employee is dealing with conflict, they usually aren't doing it alone; everyone who works with them has to deal with it in one way or another.

Higher Employee Turnover Rates

Unhappy employees are not likely to stick with a job for very long, even if the benefits and pay are attractive. Human beings can only tolerate conflict for so long. If you find your employee turnover is higher than normal and there seems to be no explanation, look at how your staff interacts with one another. Chances are there may be a bad apple in the bunch who is spoiling things for everyone else.

One way to handle employee conflict is to educate your staff about ways they can eliminate negativity from their lives. You can also handle employee differences through scheduling, transfers, or providing opportunities to air their grievances and get issues resolved. In the event this doesn't work, don't be afraid to let bad apples go before they permanent damage to your organization!

Damage to Your Brand

Be aware your brand can suffer as a result of conflict. The most common way is through your employees' interaction with the public.

Unless they are incredibly skilled at handling conflict, it can seep into dealings with stakeholders. Chances are there will be times when they are rude due to stress or they may otherwise fail to handle a situation properly.

This could cause you to lose business! It also means those treated poorly may tell others about their negative experience. Word of mouth advertising is incredibly powerful; it can work to your advantage and disadvantage.

Do what you can to manage workplace conflict effectively and quickly. When you spot a problem, cope with it immediately before it negatively affects your business.

INDIRECT COSTS OF EMPLOYEE CONFLICT

When you measure the cost of conflict within your business, there are two main areas that need to be considered—the direct and indirect costs. Both may have a trickle-down effect, where they start out as hardly noticeable and then, before you know it, you've got a serious problem on your hands.

It is important to understand the direct and indirect costs of employee conflict to your organization. This will help your leadership team develop strategies to deal with these costs, as well as handle the actual conflict itself.

Employee Absences

When employees are dealing with conflict on their own, avoidance is a common strategy. This is human nature. When you know you're going to have to deal with someone who is making you miserable, you will find ways to avoid being around that person. When that someone is a fellow employee, avoiding them translates into neglected tasks and increased employee absences.

If you offer paid sick time, this will undermine your profits. While it's one thing to provide this benefit when an employee is actually sick, it is something different if they are simply avoiding conflict at work; you are, in  effect, enabling their avoidance behavior and paying them at the same time! The costs can increase quickly, especially if you have more than one employee who is experiencing conflict.

Reduced Productivity

Employees who are thinking about problems with co-workers are not focused on their work. This results in reduced productivity. They avoid their work, even though they are physically present on the job. The employee may feel the need to "escape" every once in a while, but these small breaks generally add up to a lot of time away from their workstation.

Actual absences from work also translate into reduced productivity. Projects get delayed, excuses have to be made, and stakeholders are kept waiting. This can be disastrous to your company, particularly if you do not address the issue as quickly.

Turnover Rates

Turnover rates are typically linked to unresolved employee conflict. If an employee feels that management is helping to resolve work-related issues, he or she may be inclined to leave the organization. It is only natural for someone to want to feel secure in their workplace; if they lose the feeling of security, they may look for other employment opportunities.

The reputation of a company with excessive turnover rates gets around quickly! Once it does, finding new employees can become increasingly difficult. You may not actually hear what former employees are saying, but that doesn't mean that they aren't talking about their negative experiences with your organization. If conflict continues in your company, it may become incredibly difficult for you to find people interested in working for you, no matter what pay or benefits you offer.

Indirect costs may not affect you right away, but they will multiply over time. Don't wait for conflict to resolve itself; instead, meet these issues head on and develop a conflict management strategy. It just may save your company from ruin.

What indirect costs of employee conflict exist in my organization?

_____

_____

_____

_____

_____

_____

Which employees do I believe may be involved in indirect cost losses?

_____

_____

_____

_____

_____

_____

What general strategies might I use to stop indirect cost losses?

_____

_____

_____

_____

_____

_____

What strategies might I use to deal with specific employees to stop indirect cost losses?

_____

_____

_____

_____

_____

_____

What do I think are the causes of the conflicts that result in indirect cost losses?

_____

_____

_____

_____

_____

_____

What internal and/or external resources will I need to reduce or eliminate indirect cost losses caused by conflict?

_____

_____

_____

_____

_____

What is my timeline for reducing any indirect cost loss problems that exist?

_____

_____

_____

_____

_____

_____

DIRECT COSTS OF EMPLOYEE CONFLICT

Now let's look at the details about the direct costs of employee conflict. These are the costs that add up very quickly and can be quite significant.

Complaint Activity

The old adage, "Time is money," certainly applies here. When you let conflict go past the point of no return, you are going to have to spend a lot of time on clean-up. This time would be better spent managing your business and keeping your customers/clients happy. Every hour spent handling an issue that has escalated out of control is money coming directly out of your pocket.

Once you start looking at employee conflict in this light, you can begin to see just how costly this is. While it does initially take time and money to set up the resources to handle conflict, it will cost you much less in the end. Another adage definitely applies here: "An ounce of prevention is worth a pound of cure."

Litigation

Litigation is a term business owner never want to hear. When serious employee conflict (e.g., sexual harassment, bias, or racial tension) is not addressed, litigation may become a significant problem. If your organization did nothing to help the affected employee, you may be held liable.

Litigation can easily run into the millions of dollars, particularly in cases of sexual harassment. Even if you do have insurance coverage for your business, chances are it is not going to be enough. It is even more likely, your organization will not withstand this kind of bad publicity, even if you do have proper insurance coverage.

Reduced Sales

Reduced sales can be the biggest cause of low profit. This may result from of a lack of employee productivity. If your employees are not meeting their goals or are not focusing on their customers, the business/client relationship will suffer. Most people do not have the time or patience to deal with a company that does not have its act together. In today's competitive market place, you have to be on point 24 hours a day—no matter what.

Once you have a bad reputation in your community, for whatever reason, you are going to find it very difficult to recover. Even your most devoted customers may decide they want to do business with a proactive employer, not an employer who lets things slide. You can end up literally losing everything as the result of employee conflict if it is not addressed promptly and appropriately.

What direct costs of employee conflict exist in my organization?

_____

_____

_____

_____

_____

_____

Which employees do I believe may be involved in direct cost losses?

_____

_____

_____

_____

_____

What general strategies might I use in order to stop direct cost losses?

_____

_____

_____

_____

_____

What strategies might I use to deal with specific employees in order to stop direct cost losses?

_____

_____

_____

_____

_____

_____

What do I think are the causes of the conflicts that result in direct cost losses?

_____

_____

_____

_____

_____

_____

What internal and/or external resources will I need to reduce or eliminate direct cost losses caused by conflict?

_____

_____

_____

_____

_____

_____

What is my timeline for reducing any direct cost loss problems that exist?

_____

_____

_____

_____

_____

WHAT OTHER KINDS OF CONFLICT MIGHT YOU EXPERIENCE?

As we have worked with organizations going through major changes, we have found there are many things that need attention—things a leader may not think need attention. Every organization has systems in place that can and will be compromised by someone wishing them harm.

Financial Systems

You need to make certain your accounting systems are being monitored by your most trusted people. How much confidence do you have in your most trusted people? Is one person handling all the financial transactions for your business? What checks and balances are in place to monitor what that person is doing?

For instance, we have seen staff members responsible for generating invoices to clients use non-company invoices where payments are made to phony businesses setup by those staff members. We have seen people in charge of financial systems have checks sent to either phony companies or companies where the person signing checks has an arrangement to get a "kickback."

I was a consultant for an organization where a purchasing agent in charge of sending flowers to ill staff members was caught sending flowers  to family members for birthdays, anniversaries, and illnesses. There was no audit system in place to require a second signature be included on this type of transaction. The purchasing agent was terminated immediately.

I know of instances where bookkeepers have taken cash payments from clients and have either not entered those transactions into the accounting system or only entered partial payments. They pocketed the rest. A cash-based business needs daily monitoring and reporting to someone other than the person receiving the cash.

Do you have a petty cash system where receipts are not required in order to pay something out? This is a great way to regularly lose money.

What financial systems, if any, do I think might be compromised in my organization?

_____

_____

_____

_____

_____

If I believe my financial systems are being compromised, who might be involved?

_____

_____

_____

_____

_____

_____

What do I believe may have allowed my financial systems to be compromised?

_____

_____

_____

_____

_____

_____

What strategies might I use in order to reduce or eliminate financial system losses?

_____

_____

_____

_____

_____

_____

What internal or external resources will I need in order to reduce or eliminate financial system losses caused by conflict?

_____

_____

_____

_____

_____

What is my timeline for resolving any financial system loss problems that exist?

_____

_____

_____

_____

_____

_____

Technology Systems

How secure are your technology systems? Do you have reason to believe things you have written in emails are being shared with people other than those to whom the email was sent? Technology directors in most businesses know all they need to know about intercepting email to everyone in the organization. Are all of your important document files backed up in secure places outside of the physical environment of your business?

Some leaders think that because they have backed up documents, those documents are protected. They may be protected from simple loss or corruption, but they are not necessarily protected from technology savvy people who know where original and backup files are stored and can delete, modify, or completely destroy your files.

What technology systems, if any, do I think might be compromised in my organization?

_____

_____

_____

_____

_____

_____

If I believe my technology systems are being compromised, who might be involved?

_____

_____

_____

_____

_____

_____

What do I believe may have allowed your technology systems to be compromised?

_____

_____

_____

_____

_____

_____

What strategies might I use to reduce or eliminate technology system losses?

_____

_____

_____

_____

_____

_____

What internal or external resources will I need in order to reduce or eliminate technology system losses caused by conflict?

_____

_____

_____

_____

_____

_____

What is my timeline for resolving any technology system loss problems that exist?

_____

_____

_____

_____

_____

_____

Stealing Time

I worked with an organization once where a disgruntled employee didn't show up for work for an entire week. He had another disgruntled employee punch his time card in and out each day to make it appear as if he worked every day.

Who verifies that the times marked on a timecard are actual times worked? This dishonest procedure of punching in and out for one another could be done by every disgruntled employee. They may get away with this form of stealing if there is no verification system. Even if entire days' worth of time are not being stolen from your business, employees can check in late or leave early and no one would know the difference without a verification system in place.

Who, if anyone, do I believe may be stealing time from my organization?

_____

_____

_____

_____

What strategies might I use to prevent employees from stealing time?

_____

_____

_____

_____

What internal or external resources do I need in order to prevent employees from stealing time?

_____

_____

_____

_____

_____

What is my timeline for putting systems into place to prevent employees from stealing time?

_____

_____

_____

_____

_____

_____

Stealing Property

We have all heard stories of employees who take home a ream of paper or a box of paperclips. Such employees believe such behavior is minor and won't cause any alarms to go off. But what if most of your employees did this on a regular basis? A dollar here, a dollar there and soon it begins to accumulate to a lot of money lost to your business.

You may have heard of the fictional company where security guards checked employees before they went home each day. One man left each day with his lunch box, a briefcase, and an empty wheelbarrow. His lunch box and briefcase were checked each day and nothing was ever found. Eventually the company realized the man was stealing wheelbarrows! Businesses should never overlook the obvious.

Once I consulted with an organization where a purchasing agent sometimes picked up orders for the business. The vice president began looking for a new data projector that had been ordered, picked up by the purchasing agent, and stored in the equipment room. The vice president discovered a five-year-old data projector in the equipment room, not the new projector that had been recently ordered. We ultimately discovered the purchasing agent was taking the new equipment the business was buying and replacing it with older equipment he personally owned. We found 15 pieces of substituted equipment amounting to $16,500. The purchasing agent was terminated, charges were filed, and he was sentenced to a year in prison.

Who, if anyone, do I believe may be stealing property from my organization?

_____

_____

_____

_____

_____

_____

What strategies might I use to prevent employees from stealing property?

_____

_____

_____

_____

_____

_____

What internal or external resources do I need in order to prevent employees from stealing property?

_____

_____

_____

_____

_____

_____

What is my timeline for putting systems into place to prevent employees from stealing property?

_____

_____

_____

_____

_____

_____

OTHER CONFLICTS/LOSSES TO CONSIDER

What other problems do I anticipate having if I decide to proceed with changing the culture and structure of my organization?

_____
_____
_____
_____
_____
_____

Referring back to an earlier section in this workbook, who do I believe the 30% of non-supportive employees in my organization might be?

_____
_____
_____
_____
_____
_____

What kinds of disruptions these might non-supportive employees cause?

_____
_____
_____
_____
_____
_____

What strategies might I use to deal with disruptive/non-supportive employees?

_____

_____

_____

_____

_____

Other than non-supportive employees, what other kinds of disruptions might I expect?

_____

_____

_____

_____

What strategies might I need to use to decrease or eliminate these disruptions?

_____

_____

_____

_____

What resources might I need to help resolve organizational disruptions from both non-supportive employee and other types of disruptions?

_____

_____

_____

_____

If I decide to implement a cultural shift in my organization, where will I find employees to replace any workers who leave?

_____

_____

_____

_____

What else do I need to consider before making the final decision to proceed with changing the culture and structure in my organization?

_____

_____

_____

_____

NOTES

_____

_____

_____

_____

_____

_____

_____

_____

_____

_____

_____

_____

_____

_____

_____

_____

_____

_____

_____

_____

_____

_____

_____

_____

_____

NEXT!

Implementing Steps

IMPLEMENTING STEPS

Part 5 in a Series of 5

Before I make my final decision about making the change in my organization's culture and structure, consider the following:

Am I prepared to make a strong personal commitment to the change?

    Yes   No

Am I ready to face the variety of disruptions to my organization?

    Yes   No

Do I have the financial resources needed to make cultural changes?

    Yes   No

Am I prepared for the casualties that may happen during/after the change?

    Yes   No

WHAT ARE THE NECESSARY STEPS AND TIMELINES FOR THE CHANGE IN YOUR ORGANIZATION'S CULTURE AND STRUCTURE?

Insert each specific step and expected date for each step. (Use additional paper if needed.)

#	Step	Date
1		
2		
3		
4		
5		
6		
7		
8		
9		
10		
11		
12		
13		
14		
15		
16		
17		
18		
19		
20		

Review the steps you just completed to be certain they are in priority order.

#	Step	Date
1		
2		
3		
4		
5		
6		
7		
8		
9		
10		
11		
12		
13		
14		
15		
16		
17		
18		
19		
20		

SHOULD YOU IMPLEMENT A CHANGE IN YOUR ORGANIZATION'S CULTURE AND STRUCTURE?

Now that you have read the narrative about changing the culture and structure of an organization and have completed all the exercises provided, you should be able to decide whether or not to change the culture and structure of your organization. We have systematically guided you through all the considerations so that you can make an informed decision. After considering all the information assembled, you can use the steps provided in this workbook as a guide to implementation.

STEP 1—Work with Board of Directors to ensure support and agreement with making a change.

Timeline for Completion: _____

Tasks Required to Complete This Step

_____

_____

_____

_____

_____

_____

_____

Other Notes

_____

_____

_____

_____

_____

_____

_____

_____

_____

_____

_____

STEP 2—Start working with your leadership team on understanding why and what needs to change.

Timeline for Completion: _____

Tasks Required to Complete This Step

_____

_____

_____

_____

_____

_____

_____

Other Notes

_____

_____

_____

_____

_____

_____

_____

_____

_____

_____

_____

_____

STEP 3—Designate the responsibilities that team members will have throughout the change process.

Timeline for Completion: _____

Tasks Required to Complete This Step

_____
_____
_____
_____
_____
_____
_____

Other Notes

_____
_____
_____
_____
_____
_____
_____
_____
_____
_____
_____

STEP 4—Begin to notify customers/clients of new products and services, and the timeline for when these will be available.

Timeline for Completion: _____

Tasks Required to Complete This Step

_____

_____

_____

_____

_____

_____

_____

Other Notes

_____

_____

_____

_____

_____

_____

_____

_____

_____

_____

_____

_____

_____

STEP 5—Finalize the organization's new vision, mission statement, and values.

Timeline for Completion: _____

Tasks Required to Complete This Step

_____
_____
_____
_____
_____
_____
_____
_____

Other Notes

_____
_____
_____
_____
_____
_____
_____
_____
_____
_____
_____
_____
_____

STEP 6—Get approval from the Board of Directors of the new vision, mission statement, and values.

Timeline for Completion: _____

Tasks Required to Complete This Step

_____

_____

_____

_____

_____

_____

_____

_____

Other Notes

_____

_____

_____

_____

_____

_____

_____

_____

_____

_____

_____

_____

STEP 7—Get approval from the Board of Directors for any additional resources you will need to implement the changes. These resources may include financial, equipment, personnel, consultants, and/or legal.

Timeline for Completion: _____

Tasks Required to Complete This Step

_____
_____
_____
_____
_____
_____
_____
_____

Other Notes

_____
_____
_____
_____
_____
_____
_____
_____
_____
_____
_____
_____

STEP 8—Get approval from the Board of Directors of new policies and procedures that will be put in place.

Timeline for Completion: _____

Tasks Required to Complete This Step

_____
_____
_____
_____
_____
_____
_____
_____

Other Notes

_____
_____
_____
_____
_____
_____
_____
_____
_____
_____
_____
_____
_____

STEP 9—Actively begin to look for potential replacements for employees who may leave as a result of changes in the organization.

Timeline for Completion: _____

Tasks Required to Complete This Step

_____

_____

_____

_____

_____

_____

_____

_____

Other Notes

_____

_____

_____

_____

_____

_____

_____

_____

_____

_____

_____

_____

STEP 10—Consider using tools to assess what leadership traits and characteristics you and members of your leadership team possess. Determine if changes in leadership styles will be compatible with dealing with employees during this time of change.

Timeline for Completion: _____

Tasks Required to Complete This Step

_____
_____
_____
_____
_____
_____
_____
_____

Other Notes

_____
_____
_____
_____
_____
_____
_____
_____
_____
_____

STEP 11—Prepare the information that needs to be shared with employees. Keep in mind you do NOT want to implement ALL CHANGES immediately. Plan to move slowly and carefully.

Timeline for Completion: _____

Tasks Required to Complete This Step

_____

_____

_____

_____

_____

_____

_____

Other Notes

_____

_____

_____

_____

_____

_____

_____

_____

_____

_____

_____

STEP 12—Identify the most trusted employees in your organization. Inform them of the changes that are going to be implemented and ensure that all employees are informed of the new vision, mission statement, and values.

Timeline for Completion: _____

Tasks Required to Complete This Step

_____

_____

_____

_____

_____

_____

_____

Other Notes

_____

_____

_____

_____

_____

_____

_____

_____

_____

_____

STEP 13—Hold information sessions for employees and give them a chance to ask questions. Be sure to explain in detail the reasons for the organizational changes.

Timeline for Completion: _____

Tasks Required to Complete This Step

_____

_____

_____

_____

_____

_____

_____

Other Notes

_____

_____

_____

_____

_____

_____

_____

_____

_____

_____

_____

_____

STEP 14—Be prepared to answer questions about policies, layoffs, changes in salaries and benefits, new products and services, and the timeline for when the changes will be implemented.

Timeline for Completion: _____

Tasks Required to Complete This Step

_____

_____

_____

_____

_____

_____

_____

_____

Other Notes

_____

_____

_____

_____

_____

_____

_____

_____

_____

_____

_____

_____

STEP 15—If new training is needed for employees, begin the training process as soon as possible. Outside trainers, rather than inside resources, are usually more successful in getting employees to accept new ideas.

Timeline for Completion: _____

Tasks Required to Complete This Step

_____

_____

_____

_____

_____

_____

_____

_____

Other Notes

_____

_____

_____

_____

_____

_____

_____

_____

_____

_____

_____

_____

STEP 16—If new equipment is needed to implement the changes, place the orders in accordance with the organization's purchasing policies.

Timeline for Completion: _____

Tasks Required to Complete This Step

_____

_____

_____

_____

_____

_____

_____

Other Notes

_____

_____

_____

_____

_____

_____

_____

_____

_____

_____

_____

_____

STEP 17—Put into place any protection systems needed. These may include financial, technology, and theft of time and/or property systems. Be sure this is completed as soon as the changes begin.

Timeline for Completion: _____

Tasks Required to Complete This Step

_____
_____
_____
_____
_____
_____
_____
_____

Other Notes

_____
_____
_____
_____
_____
_____
_____
_____
_____
_____
_____
_____

STEP 18—Ensure that you and other members of your leadership team are visible and available to employees as the changes are put into place.

Timeline for Completion: _____

Tasks Required to Complete This Step

_____
_____
_____
_____
_____
_____
_____
_____

Other Notes

_____
_____
_____
_____
_____
_____
_____
_____
_____
_____
_____
_____
_____

STEP 19—Meet with your leadership team to discuss what is being heard and witnessed about the changes.

Timeline for Completion: _____

Tasks Required to Complete This Step

_____
_____
_____
_____
_____
_____
_____
_____

Other Notes

_____
_____
_____
_____
_____
_____
_____
_____
_____
_____
_____
_____
_____

STEP 20—Meet with your most trusted employees to discuss what is being heard and witnessed about the changes.

Timeline for Completion: _____

Tasks Required to Complete This Step

_____

_____

_____

_____

_____

_____

_____

Other Notes

_____

_____

_____

_____

_____

_____

_____

_____

_____

_____

_____

_____

STEP 21—Meet with any employees who are unhappy about the changes and who are willing to discuss their concerns with you or their immediate supervisors.

Timeline for Completion: _____

Tasks Required to Complete This Step

_____

_____

_____

_____

_____

_____

_____

Other Notes

_____

_____

_____

_____

_____

_____

_____

_____

_____

_____

_____

STEP 22—Check your timeline to see if you are meeting benchmarks as planned. Make adjustments as necessary, ensuring that changes are made slowly and in an orderly manner.

Timeline for Completion: _____

Tasks Required to Complete This Step

_____

_____

_____

_____

_____

_____

_____

Other Notes

_____

_____

_____

_____

_____

_____

_____

_____

_____

_____

STEP 23—Reward or praise those who are actively supporting the changes.

Timeline for Completion: _____

Tasks Required to Complete This Step

_____

_____

_____

_____

_____

_____

_____

_____

Other Notes

_____

_____

_____

_____

_____

_____

_____

_____

_____

_____

_____

_____

_____

STEP 24—Have the leadership team identify anyone who is unsure of whether to support the changes but is not causing any disruptions to the change process.

Timeline for Completion: _____

Tasks Required to Complete This Step

_____
_____
_____
_____
_____
_____
_____
_____

Other Notes

_____
_____
_____
_____
_____
_____
_____
_____
_____
_____
_____

STEP 25—Meet individually or in small groups with those who were identified by your leadership team in the previous step.

Timeline for Completion: _____

Tasks Required to Complete This Step

_____
_____
_____
_____
_____
_____
_____
_____

Other Notes

_____
_____
_____
_____
_____
_____
_____
_____
_____
_____
_____

STEP 26—Be sure you are visible and available to all employees on a regular basis. Do not leave this entirely to your leadership team. Ask employees how they are doing with the changes, inquire about any problems they are experiencing, and ask for any suggestions they might have.

Timeline for Completion: _____

Tasks Required to Complete This Step

_____

_____

_____

_____

_____

_____

_____

Other Notes

_____

_____

_____

_____

_____

_____

_____

_____

_____

_____

STEP 27—Document in detail all employee issues that are causing disruption to the change process. Meet and discuss individual employee problems as soon as they occur. Document in writing and detail the results of the meeting(s).

Timeline for Completion: _____

Tasks Required to Complete This Step

_____

_____

_____

_____

_____

_____

_____

_____

Other Notes

_____

_____

_____

_____

_____

_____

_____

_____

_____

_____

STEP 28—If/when an employee causes problems that are serious enough to consider termination, meet with legal counsel to ensure all policies and due process steps are being followed. In some cases when a termination takes place, it is advisable to have legal counsel present when the employee is notified. In other cases, it may not be possible to have counsel present. In those cases, it is advisable to wait until the end of the work day, meet with the employee, have a member of your leadership team present with you, notify the employee of the termination, have them return their keys to the building, and walk them out.

Timeline for Completion: _____

Tasks Required to Complete This Step

_____
_____
_____
_____
_____
_____
_____
_____

Other Notes

_____
_____
_____
_____
_____
_____

STEP 29—Have a terminated employee's supervisor establish an appointment with the employee in order for the employee to remove their PERSONAL ITEMS from the building. The supervisor should remain with the employee at all times while in the building.

Timeline for Completion: _____

Tasks Required to Complete This Step

_____

_____

_____

_____

_____

_____

_____

Other Notes

_____

_____

_____

_____

_____

_____

_____

_____

_____

_____

STEP 30—Have a terminated employee's records removed from their office and have the person removed from all technology systems. Be sure to back up files they accessed during their employment.

Timeline for Completion: _____

Tasks Required to Complete This Step

_____
_____
_____
_____
_____
_____
_____
_____

Other Notes

_____
_____
_____
_____
_____
_____
_____
_____
_____
_____
_____
_____

STEP 31—Interview replacements for terminated employees. Follow policies and procedures for hiring new employees. Follow suggestions of legal counsel before advertising and/or hiring new employees.

Timeline for Completion: _____

Tasks Required to Complete This Step

_____
_____
_____
_____
_____
_____
_____

Other Notes

_____
_____
_____
_____
_____
_____
_____
_____
_____
_____

STEP 32—Meet with new employees to review the job description, vision, mission statement, and values of the organization. Provide whatever training a new employee might need in order to be integrated smoothly into the organization.

Timeline for Completion: _____

Tasks Required to Complete This Step

_____
_____
_____
_____
_____
_____
_____
_____

Other Notes

_____
_____
_____
_____
_____
_____
_____
_____
_____
_____
_____

STEP 33—The Leadership Team Supervisor should meet frequently with new employees to ensure they are not being influenced by unhappy employees. Use positive reinforcement with new employees and encourage loyalty to the organization.

Timeline for Completion: _____

Tasks Required to Complete This Step

_____

_____

_____

_____

_____

_____

_____

_____

Other Notes

_____

_____

_____

_____

_____

_____

_____

_____

_____

_____

STEP 34—Add new employees to the technology systems of the organization and train them on the proper use of the systems.

Timeline for Completion: _____

Tasks Required to Complete This Step

_____

_____

_____

_____

_____

_____

_____

Other Notes

_____

_____

_____

_____

_____

_____

_____

_____

_____

_____

_____

_____

STEP 35—Maintain on-going communications with ALL EMPLOYEES regarding the changes. Keep them informed of the status of established timelines. Continue to invite individuals to meet with you to discuss any ideas or concerns they might have.

Timeline for Completion: _____

Tasks Required to Complete This Step

_____

_____

_____

_____

_____

_____

_____

_____

Other Notes

_____

_____

_____

_____

_____

_____

_____

_____

_____

_____

STEP 36—Regularly hold ALL EMPLOYEE staff meetings where they can ask questions, get answers, and be updated on the change process in a safe environment.

Timeline for Completion: _____

Tasks Required to Complete This Step

_____

_____

_____

_____

_____

_____

_____

_____

Other Notes

_____

_____

_____

_____

_____

_____

_____

_____

_____

_____

_____

_____

STEP 37—Use the REGULARLY SCHEDULED meetings of the Board of Directors to keep them informed of the changes being implemented and the status of the timeline benchmarks put into place prior to the start of the changes. Get approval from the Board of Directors for any new policies and/or procedures that might be needed but were not foreseen. Hold SPECIAL MEETINGS in cases of emergency. Follow the OPEN MEETING LAWS regarding prior notice of such a meeting.

Timeline for Completion: _____

Tasks Required to Complete This Step

_____

_____

_____

_____

_____

_____

_____

_____

Other Notes

_____

_____

_____

_____

_____

_____

_____

_____

STEP 38—If your organization is an entity receiving public funding, state or federal tax dollars, be certain that you are reporting in town hall meetings and other forms of public information vehicles what is taking place in the organization. Report regularly to ensure that any disgruntled or terminated employees are not disseminating false information about the organization, you, or your leadership team.

Timeline for Completion: _____

Tasks Required to Complete This Step

_____
_____
_____
_____
_____
_____
_____
_____

Other Notes

_____
_____
_____
_____
_____
_____
_____
_____

STEP 39—Expect the unexpected. No matter how carefully you have planned for all contingencies, things will happen where no plan, policy, or procedure is in place. Before taking action, analyze what is needed. Avoid acting too quickly; this often results in poor decisions.

Timeline for Completion: _____

Tasks Required to Complete This Step

_____
_____
_____
_____
_____
_____
_____
_____

Other Notes

_____
_____
_____
_____
_____
_____
_____
_____
_____
_____

STEP 40—Celebrate success along the way. Reward and/or acknowledge the work of employees who are helping to make the changes successful.

Timeline for Completion: _____

Tasks Required to Complete This Step

_____

_____

_____

_____

_____

_____

_____

Other Notes

_____

_____

_____

_____

_____

_____

_____

_____

_____

_____

_____

_____

_____

Thank you for purchasing this book and using it to help you analyze and plan for potential cultural changes in your organization. Feel free to contact us at any time.

Dr. Dennis R. Clodi

Dr. Dennis Clodi spent 32 years in public education as a teacher, principal, and superintendent. An adjunct professor for two universities since 2003, he is an expert in leadership and management, organizational change, communication strategies, problem identification and action plan development, school finance, and grant writing.

Dennis has been CEO of three successful Internet Service Provider companies serving nine rural communities. He was also President and CEO of a successful computer sales and service company. In 2003, Dennis sold these successful companies to allow more time to for him to do consulting and professional development training for companies such as UPS, Federal Express, Sears, Alberto Culver, as well as other community organizations and school districts.

An author and editor, Dennis has an M. Ed. in Educational leadership from the University of Illinois and an Ed. D. Degree from Illinois State University. With a 20-million dollar grant, he designed and delivered professional development training to over 8,000 teachers on the topic "Designing Engaged Learning Instruction and Technology Activities in K-12 classrooms."

Dennis has been an entrepreneur since the age of 13. Being a skilled ventriloquist allowed him to earn enough money to pay for his bachelor's degree. His performances on TV and Radio provided him the opportunity to travel throughout Canada, promoting tourism in America and sport fishing in Florida.

Dr. Clodi is a certified substance abuse trainer for trainers and the author of a communications manual for parents, *Mountain Education: The answer to the 3 D's—Drinking, Driving, and Drugs* is a Subject Matter Expert with Professional Progress Academy. He can be reached at d9clo43di14@gmail.com

> *An assumption that everyone in your organization knows and understands your organization's Vision, Mission, & Philosophy will likely lead to organizational failure."*
>
> *—Dr. Dennis R. Clodi*
> *815.939.7905 d9clo43di14@gmail.com*

DR. RICH SCHUTTLER

Dr. Rich Schuttler a customer-driven & quality-focused innovative and engaging international public speaker, educator, and author. He has 30-years of diversified, domestic and international management and leadership improvement expertise within academic, federal/state governments, and Fortune 1,000 environments developing strategies and implementation methods. Dr. Rich has mentored executives, faculty, and students from around the world in a variety of professional leadership and management settings. Rich served in the *U.S. Navy* and retired after 23 years of honorable service in the field of cryptology and earned his Ph.D. in *Applied Management and Decision Sciences* from Walden University. Dr. Schuttler is the author of Best Selling book *Laws of Communication: The Intersection Where Leadership Meets Employee Performance and Everyday Leader Heroes: 10 Leadership Characteristics in Everyday People.* Dr. Rich Schuttler is the CEO & Co-Founder of *Professional Progress Academy,* an online membership training and education site. Dr. Schuttler and Dr. Ruby Rouse have developed a communications survey tool and consulting service for leaders of organizations. The SLCI tool can be accessed at: http://www.drrichschuttler.com/slci-mini-test.htm

602.541.2498 drrich@drrichschuttler.com

Economist Intelligence Unit. (2004). *Strategy execution: Achieving operational excellence.* Retrieved from http://graphics.eiu.com/files/ad_pdfs/Celeran_EIU_WP.pdf.

Kaplan, R. S., & Norton, D. P. (2001). *The Strategy-Focused Organization: How Balanced Scorecard Companies Thrive in the New Business Environment.* Boston: Harvard Business School Press.

Moorcroft, D. (2003, October/November) Linking communication strategy with organizational goals. *Strategic Communication Management, 7(6),* 24-27.

Schuttler, R. A. (2010). *Laws of Communications.* Hoboken, NJ: Wiley

www.ingramcontent.com/pod-product-compliance
Lightning Source LLC
Chambersburg PA
CBHW022006170526
45157CB00003B/1174